A. M. D. G.

A Safe View of Spiritism for Catholics

BY

REV. JOSEPH C. SASIA, S. J.

Published with Approval of Ecclesiastical Authority.

FOR FREE DISTRIBUTION.

1920
POPP & HOGAN, PRINTERS
San Jose, California.

Office of the ARCHBISHOP, San Francisco, California.

Nihil Obstat, J. M. BYRNE, Censor Deputatus.

Imprimi Potest, MSGR. PATRICK L. RYAN, Vicar General.

April 28, 1920.

In the interest of creating a more extensive selection of rare historical book reprints, we have chosen to reproduce this title even though it may possibly have occasional imperfections such as missing and blurred pages, missing text, poor pictures, markings, dark backgrounds and other reproduction issues beyond our control. Because this work is culturally important, we have made it available as a part of our commitment to protecting, preserving and promoting the world's literature. Thank you for your understanding.

FOREWORD

The timeliness of this little pamphlet is due to the fact that Spiritism is of late displaying an increased activity, a menace to the religion, mental sanity, and moral character of Christian believers. Its title shows that the appeal is chiefly directed to Catholics; but we feel inclined to think that non-Catholics also may read it with profit. The **Imprimatur** kindly granted by the Church Authority of this Archdiocese affords to the readers a sure guarantee of the soundness of the views expressed in its pages. To facilitate its diffusion among our people, a generous Catholic Lady of San Jose has kindly volunteered to defray the expenses of its publication; hence it is intended to be distributed free. Should this small brochure prove beneficial, as we earnestly hope, to those that will peruse it, the author will deem himself to be thus amply compensated for the labor spent in writing it.

JOSEPH C. SASIA, S. J.

Librarian
Santa Clara University
June, 1920.

444162

"Put you on the armor of God, that you may be able to stand against the deceits of the devil. For our wrestling is not against flesh and blood, but against principalities and powers, against the rulers of the world of this darkness, against the spirits of wickedness in the high places."

Ephesians VI, 11-12.

A Safe View of Spiritism for Catholics.

FIRST ARTICLE

Introduction.

On the Paramount Importance of the Subject Treated.

I.

Spiritism is the name properly given to the belief that the living can and do communicate with the spirits or souls of the departed. Its main purpose is to ascertain what is their experience beyond the grave, and to find out whether it corresponds with the teachings of Christianity both as regards this life and the next. Another object is also to satisfy the curiosity of inquirers concerning the knowledge of other secret things.

This practice of consulting the dead is **generally** carried out through the intervention of the so-called mediums, living persons, who are said to be more or less susceptible to the influence of the supposed spirits of the dead, and they act as intermediaries in receiving and transmitting their communications. We advisedly say **generally**, for, as will be shown in the sequel, the presence of a medium is not absolutely necessary for the evocation of spiritistic manifestations.

Though such performances are also designated by the word spiritualism, yet, to avoid confusion, it is better to reserve said term to signify the philosophical doctrine, which holds that there exists a spiritual order of beings no less real than the material, and in particular that the human soul is a spiritual and therefore intelligent and immortal substance.

Modern spiritism within a generation has passed beyond the limits of a merely popular movement, mainly prompted by sentimental curiosity, to serious inquiry, and as such has challenged the attention of the upholders of Christianity, and of the scientific world. On this account it is becoming every day unceasingly impossible for any educated person to dismiss the subject of spiritism with mere contempt. Owing to these and other considerations, a few articles have been prepared by the writer for the readers of the Mercury Herald, which its able editor has kindly consented to publish in four successive issues.

The present introductory essay is intended to answer the following preliminary questions:

1—What are the chief spiritistic phenomena?
2—Should we accept many of them as true, genuine facts?
3—How can they be rationally accounted for?

Some belong to the physical or material order of things while others must be ascribed to intellectual agencies, whatever they may be.

1. Physical Facts. Objects, which could hardly be moved by several men, are easily lifted and transported instantaneously from remote distances by the medium. Musical instruments are played without being touched by any one. Heavy bodies are seen suspended and floating in the air without any visible support. The alteration of weight of bodies from eight pounds to forty pounds, a fact testified by an eminent scientist, the late Sir William Crookes, who wrote: "I had the entire management of this experimental trial, employed an instrument of great accuracy and took every care to exclude the possibility of trickery." Dr. H. Carrington bears testimony to the opposite phenomenon, the loss of weight. He writes: "During the experiments in Milan it was found that the medium in about twenty seconds had lost no less than seventeen pounds."

But what is considered the triumph of spiritism is the wonder of materialization, which consists in the actual appearance in its full bodily form of a supposed discarnate soul, that moves about clothed in a kind of silk drapery, speaks to the sitters in audible whispers, and, after a time, gradually melts away before their eyes.

The mediums give answers, which absolutely exceed the well-known limits of their culture, they speak ancient and modern languages at the bidding of the experimenters, solve intricate mathematical problems and perform other feats which only a superior intelligence could accomplish. The following is a case in point:

The great English astronomer, the late John F. Herschel, at first called spiritism sheer quackery. A friend of his invited him to a seance to be held in clear daylight so as to exclude any attempt at trickery or jugglery of any kind. The medium purposely chosen was a country woman utterly destitute of education. As soon as she had fallen into the usual trance, the astronomer, bent on unmasking her, questioned her concerning certain intricate mathematical problems, which he himself had solved. She answered that the calculations of Herschel were wrong, and stated what corrections should be made.

The astronomer laughed as an unbeliever. But what happened? Some time after, going over his figures, he found that the medium was right, and he was honest enough to acknowledge his mistake in the public press.

But the wonderful feats of spiritism described above are not the exclusive doings of the educated white race. The far more marvelous achievements of the Fakirs of India prove that the whites are mere beginners and are outdone by their dusky brothers. For proof of this statement see the book entitled "Spiritism Unveiled", by D. I. Lanslot, O. S. B., Vicar Apostolic of Northern Transvaal. B. Herder, St. Louis, Mo.

If space permitted it, other similar instances might be alleged; but the preceding ones will suffice for our purpose. Are many such phenomena real facts?

2. As medicine has its quacks, science its impostors, commercial trade its frauds, so spiritism may, at times, have been found guilty of jugglery, and palmed off its trickery as genuine wonders, thus deceiving unwary and gullible folks. But this fact does not warrant sweeping denial of all the doings of spiritism. Such a conclusion would be both illogical and unfair, and would moreover brand as dishonest, mean impostors a large multitude of fair-minded witnesses of spiritistic wonders. In spite of occasional exposure, there occur phenomena, which cannot be ascribed to fraud of any sort.

This view is shared by men, whose knowledge and integrity is altogether above suspicion. The experiments they relate as eye witnesses, the severe tests, to which they have been put, the many precautions taken to avoid all possible deception, vouch with absolute certainity for the undeniable reality of spiritistic marvels. Hence we fully endorse the view of Rev. Herbert Thurston, S. J., expressed in his recent article on the peril of spiritism, published in the London Weekly Universe:

"I believe that, in spite of much trickery, astounding manifestations, which cannot be other than preternatural, casually occur. It seems to me that no human testimony can avail to establish any historical fact at all, if we are to set aside the evidence for these happenings."

Instead, therefore, of cutting off the vexatious problem by a sweeping, irrational denial, we deem it a wiser and braver course to grapple with it, and endeavor to reach a reasonable and satisfactory solution. Hence we cannot approve the conduct of certain modern scientists, who either deny the facts, which are shown to be true, or thrust them aside as unworthy of serious investigation.

The Spiritists will admit, with all level-headed men, that nobody can give what he has not, and that a reasonable cause must be assigned of Spiritism, for to resort continually to unknown causes as a justification of our ignorance, does not offer a rational explanation accounting satisfactorily for facts, the reality of which cannot be denied except by obstinate skeptics.

3. In accordance with the claims of reason and common sense, every event must have a cause; every effect calls for an efficient cause, force, or agent able to produce it. On this all are agreed, the only practical difference in the various explanations of the facts of spiritism consists in the nature of that cause.

Among the possible causes, fairly covering the whole ground, the following have been advocated by different writers, and the disciples of several spiritistic schools:

1. Almighty God Himself through the ministry of the good angels.
2. The extraordinary achievements of the medium when in a trance.
3. Some mysterious natural agent or force, the theory of some modern scientists.
4. The so-called discarnate souls of the dead as held by the upholders of spiritism.
5. The evil spirits, Satan and the fallen angels called demons, the firm belief, as will be proved, of all conservative Christians, and of all the defenders of sacred Scripture.

For clearness sake we shall adopt in this discussion in our next article the process of elimination and allege several cogent reasons why, after rejecting as unsatisfactory all other causes, the spiritistic phenomena must be attributed only, and exclusively to devilish intervention. This view fully justifies the saying of St. Peter Chrysologus: "Qui jocatur cum diabolo, non gaudebit cum Christo." "He who meddles with the devil will not rejoice with Christ."

It shall be our object to draw from reliable sources any such material as will be deemed necessary to our purpose, and also to take into consideration the current various systems of interpretation, which have been devised with a view to an explanation of the phenomena in question. The facts shown to be taking place in connection with recent experimental research are many and wonderful, and they present problems of the greatest importance and significance. It is only the earnest, unprejudiced study of them, in the light of divine revelation and sound reason, that can lead the inquiring mind to a discovery of the real agents responsible for the production of the spiritistic marvels, and thus enable it to determine the question as to the lawfulness and morality of the practice of spiritism.

SECOND ARTICLE

The True, Real Cause of Certain Spiritistic Phenomena.

II.

The purpose I have in view in penning these articles is to set forth as clearly and concisely as possible the orthodox doctrine on Spiritism; a doctrine held not only by Catholics, but also by all consistent believers in historic Christianity, where alone we find the true standard, by which the momentous problems presented by that so-called new religion can be fairly and adequately solved, and the inquiring mind led to the detection of the real agents responsible for the spiritistic marvels.

Correct View.

Such a knowledge, practically necessary in our days, will enable the reader to pronounce a correct judgment on the matter at issue, and on the teachings of the two leading spiritistic lights, Sir Oliver Lodge and Conan Doyle, a prominent English physician. The latter, in a recent public lecture, was bold enough to give to his audience the horrible advice that all should become spiritistic mediums; an advice, which the medical profession, that respects itself, will, no doubt, indignantly repudiate in the interest of health, religion and morality, menaced by Spiritism, as shown later on.

The severe tests, to which many spiritistic facts have been put and the absolute trustworthiness of the experimenters vouch with certainty for their undeniable reality. It is now my task to pass in review each of the different causes proposed as explanatory of the doings of Spiritism, so as to ascertain to which of them they should be ascribed.

Some people, struck by the astounding wonders they witnessed at the seances, thought that they were the work of the Deity. Hence the need of the inquiry:

(1) Are the phenomena of Spiritism to be attributed to God?

The simple proposal of the question suggests the answer, which is an emphatic negative. They cannot be ascribed to God's immediate agency, who certainly is not to be supposed acting as a mere tool in the hands of His creatures, to obey their summons and operate wonders at their bidding to gratify their morbid curiosity.

Moreover, has not Almighty God forbidden, under the severest penalties both temporal and eternal, the superstitious practice of consulting the dead? The Lord thus spoke to the Israelites through the prophet Moses: "Neither let it be found among you any one that consulteth pythonic spirits, or that seeketh the truth from the dead. For the Lord abhorreth these things." Deuteronomy, xviii, 11-12.

Protestant Testimony.

It is gratifying to see the orthodox doctrine fully endorsed by the following Protestant testimony: More than thirty years ago, when modern Spiritism was in its infancy, the eminent Presbyterian divine, De Witt Talmage, inveighed against it with all the force of his eloquence: "What does God think of all these delusions? He thinks so severely that He never speaks of them but with livid thunders of indignation; for all that do these things are an abomination unto the Lord. After that be a Spiritist, if you dare."

The attitude of the Catholic Church towards the practice of Spiritism is uncompromising and unmistakable, as it appears from the two following decrees of the Holy Office: "To call up the souls of the dead is a deception absolutely unlawful, heretical, and scandalous." Approved by Pius IX in 1858. To the question whether it is lawful to be present at any Spiritistic communication, even with no intention of dealing with wicked spirits, the answer was an emphatic negative and bears the sanction of the reigning Pontiff, Benedict XV, April 27, 1917.

Some wiseacres, who know as much about Spiritism as the average American about Oriental languages, think that the best solution of the vexed problem is simply to ridicule it. Our answer is that such an offhand explanation, to say nothing at present of its glaring absurdity, throws an impertinent reflection on the policy of the Catholic Church, who, instead of merely ridiculing Spiritism, thought it wise to denounce it, and assign the reasons for its condemnation.

(2) Are the facts of Spiritism to be assigned to good angels?

We take here for granted what Catholics and the generality of Christians hold concerning the holy angels, who, at their trial, remained faithful and loyal to their Sovereign Creator, and are now partakers of heavenly happiness. Being perfectly united with their Lord, and entirely submissive to His holy will, they never use their power in doing what God hates and absolutely forbids. They fight with us against the common enemies, Satan and the rebel angels, the battles of the Lord, Whose design they accomplish in our behalf. Hence it is certain that they have nothing to do with the abominable performances of the Spiritistic seances.

(3) Shall we say that the mediums themselves are the authors of the astounding feats of Spiritism?

Unscientific Explanations.

A number of scientists, particularly if materialists, determined to exclude anything preternatural, and much more the supernatural, confronted with the undeniable facts of Spiritism have devised explanations highly discreditable to science itself, because both silly and absurd. Hence they need only be stated to be refuted by any man of elementary knowledge and sound common sense. Their opinions differ so widely, and are at times so contradictory that it seems quite useless to examine them. A few specimens will suffice.

Dr. William Crookes speaks thus: "In some individuals acting as mediums there is an organism that enables them to work all the spiritistic wonders. It is called the Psychic force."

Dr. Rickert writes: "The intellectual marvels witnessed at seances are the result of the astounding knowledge hidden in the mind of mediums, and exhibited by them when in a trance."

Others, especially the materialists of the medical fraternity, attribute all those phenomena to fits of hysteria and neurasthenia or to a mysterious fluid emanating from the entranced medium. All such and similar theories are shown to be false by the fact admitted by the Spiritists themselves that all mediums, even the most clever, are simply instrumental channels of communication, entirely subject to the control and caprice of the real, though invisible authors of the phenomena in question. It is well known that, at times, such communications are suddenly interrupted; what becomes then of the psychic force, the latent knowledge and the mysterious fluid of the medium?

According to some theorists the action alone of the medium suffices to account for all spiritistic phenomena. There exists in man, they say, an astral substance of a nature between matter and spirit, which, if detached from the body of the medium affords a means of communication with the spirits. Mediumship therefore consists in the ability of a person to detach from his body this astral substance. Of the existence of this strange being as well as of the sublimal self, and automatism, the so-called natural causes of spiritistic phenomena, not a shred of proof is adduced. As to the astral substance suffice it to say that a being, which is neither spirit nor matter, is simply a non-entity.

(4) Are the phenomena of Spiritism the work of some natural force or agency hitherto unknown to science?

A Theory Upset.

The advocates of such view reason thus: "We do not know all the forces of organic and inorganic beings. Now, since science, always progressive, may discover in the course of time as a stern reality what we at present ignore, who knows but in the near future, a hidden natural agent may be discovered and the now mysterious phenomena fully explained?"

We freely grant that the future may have wonderful surprises in store for us. In fact, what was considered an impossibility a century ago, is now a reality, wireless telegraphy. There is, however, at hand a principle to guide us, which is admitted by all, namely, that no effect can be superior to the cause producing it. The unbiased inquirer cannot fail to see that blind natural forces are utterly unable to give rise to effects superior to themselves such as all the spiritistic marvels, the work not of blind, necessary agents, but of intelligent and free causes.

Common sense tells us that to speak different languages, both ancient and modern, to solve correctly intricate mathematical problems, to diagnose successfully complicated diseases cannot be the work of any natural forces however powerful they may be.

As recourse to as yet unknown physical or natural agents is the chief argument of our opponents, we deem it advisable to demonstrate at greater length its absolute worthlessness from a philosophical point of view. The answer is derived from the Civiltá Cattolica, a roman semi-monthly production designated by Mr. E. Preuss as the leading Catholic review of the world. The writer in an article on Spiritism reasons thus: According to the present order of Providence, manifested by experience and observation, whatever force or agent acts within the limits of physical nature possesses the following fixed and unchangeable characters:

First. It is determined to one only particular effect—Thus heat expands, and cold contracts, and the opposite can never occur.

Secondly. It is constant and uniform in its operations, for every natural force is governed by fixed, invariable laws.

Thirdly. When the conditions required for its activity are present, it necessarily acts. Apply a flame to powder and the explosion is inevitable.

Fourthly. In its operations it is entirely destitute of liberty or choice. Can we say that a lighted candle is free to burn or extinguish itself?

As none of these conditions are verified in the spiritistic phenomena, the observer is logically drawn to the conclusion that they cannot be abscribed to any known or unknown purely natural agency or force.

In fact, first, in the spiritistic seances are seen substantially different effects such as the physical, psychical, physiological and psychological wonders.

Secondly, there is no uniformity of action witnessed, for every operation has its own peculiar method, every method its varieties, and every variety its exceptions, all effects, which obey no constant, fixed law.

Third, when everything is ready for a spiritistic seance, are the expected manifestations always forthcoming at the bidding of the experimenter, or at the choice of the medium? By no means, for, at times, the performance must be either prolonged, or interrupted, or indefinitely postponed, on account of the caprice of the agents at work, whoever they be.

Fourthly, from what has just been said, the intellectual free action of the invisible agents is patent to all. Therefore as all the characters of the spiritistic phenomena are essentially different from those of the physical, natural forces, it stands to reason to conclude that they cannot be attributed to any natural agent.

(5) Should we then agree with the Spiritists and ascribe the facts in question to the souls of the dead?

Here also we must answer in the negative. The principal reason is because such souls are utterly unable to perform either the physical or the intellectual deeds witnessed at the seances. In fact, all physical or mechanical performances require action on matter, which is naturally impossible to discarnate souls. As St. Thomas and many Catholic philosophers hold, pure spirits, whether angels or demons, not being determined to animate any particular bodily organism, have full power, though under God's control, to act on matter and work the material feats of Spiritism.

Human souls, on the contrary, when once separated from their body by death, retain no further power of action on matter. Neither can the souls of the dead operate any of the intellectual wonders; for the astounding answers given entirely exceed the well known limits of the mental capacity, which they possessed when living.

Have the Spiritists ever proved that the mere fact of death transforms persons of average intelligence into prodigies of learning? Or shall we suppose that God Himself will infuse into departed souls the extraordinary knowledge displayed at the seances, and thus enable men to consult the dead and to do the very thing which He Himself so rigorously condemns?

Moreover, the trivialities, obscenities, blasphemies, and, at times, the expressions of hatred against the sitters are notorious and the spiritists themselves deplore their occurrence. Can these abominal things be said to be the work of departed souls, whose moral integrity in life, in some cases well known to the audience, makes them utterly incredible and absurd? That the astounding communications received at the seances do not come from the dead, but, from the fallen spirits, the demons, we learn from the spiritists themselves. Allan Kardec—formerly M. Rivail, the French standard bearer of the new cult, in his book on mediums, writes that "any question may be asked at the seance. If it is beneath the superior dignity of a superior spirit to answer, an inferior spirit will always be at hand to satisfy the curiosity of the inquirer," although, he naively remarks, they are not conspicuous for truthfulness.

We here fully endorse the words of J. Godfrey Raupert:

"Many of the best informed Catholic Theologians maintain that, when all natural explanations of the phenomena in question, such as fraud, nerves, the possibilities of telepathy, etc., have been allowed for, there are phenomena, which must be ascribed to the action of evil spirits—fallen angels—masquerading as the souls of the dead."—The Fortnightly Review, May 1, 1920.

Among the many authorities that could be alleged to maintain the Catholic view the following will suffice for the present:

Authorities for Catholic View

The famous French astronomer, Flammarion, thus replies to the Spiritists: "Their doctrine is far from being demonstrated. The innumerable observations, which I have collected during more than forty years, all prove to me the contrary. No satisfactory identification has ever been made. That human souls survive the destruction of the body by death, I have not a shadow of doubt. But that they manifest themselves by the processes employed in Spiritistic seances, there has been no absolute proof."

(6) Are the doings of Spiritism the work of Satan and of his companions, the fallen angels?

After excluding all the preceding explanations as altogether unsatisfactory there remains but one cause that fully accounts for the many spiritistic phenomena, that cannot be ascribed to mere jugglery, and that is the presence and action of wicked angels, the demons.

But here I am confronted with an apparently unsurmountable difficulty and it is this: Certain men, who are supposed to be taken seriously, do not believe at all in the existence of wicked angels. Speaking from the editorial pulpit they told us, some time ago, that Satan is a myth, and that it is impossible for believers in God to admit the existence of any so-called demons. We must be quite sure that there exist no such beings in creation, for they said it themselves. In fact they advised Mr. Stainton Moses, a famous medium "to cease to be perplexed about thoughts of imagined devils, for there is no devil or prince of devils such as theology has feigned."

But as this was said by lying spirits, we shall have to admit the contrary as true and still believe with all Christians worthy of the name in the existence and the wicked doings of demons.

Glancing over the Bible's contents, from Genesis to the Apocalypse, we find not less than fifty references to Satan and the rebel angels.

Christ's Miracle

Jesus Christ gave evidence of His Divine power by the expulsion of demons from hundreds of possessed and obsessed persons. On the theory of the non-existence of such creatures, Christ's miracles just mentioned were a huge fraud, and He actually played the hypocrite by pretending to expel devils that did not exist. No believer in the Bible can deny the existence of the wicked spirits, the devils, without stultifying himself.

In the days of the first Reformers (1600), when so many traditional doctrines were rudely called in question, the belief in the existence of fallen angels was found so deeply rooted in the Christian conscience of the Faithful that no attempt was made to deny that truth.

Dr. H. Carrington has this to say on the subject: "If anything could make me believe in the doctrine of evil, lying spirits, it would be the sittings I had, when Mrs. Piper acted as a medium. I then gained the distinct impression that, instead of the souls of the personages she claimed to be present, I was dealing with exceedingly deceitful intelligences."

Stainton Moses, quoted above, giving his own experience, said of the agent at work in a seance: "It bespeaks a deeply evil nature. Such an impostor acting with an air of sincerity must be Satan clothed in light."

Catholics can have no hesitation in their belief in the existence and nefarious activities of demons. After Holy Mass, celebrated daily in countless churches throughout the world, by order of the Vicar of Christ, a public prayer is recited to implore the divine protection, and the special assistance of the Archangel, St. Michael, against the malice and the snares of Satan and the other evil spirits who prowl about the world seeking the ruin of souls.

Several other reasons will be adduced in our next article, in which we shall speak of the many fatal dangers of Spiritism to Religion, health and morality.

It has then been shown that devilish intervention is the only true cause of all real Spiritistic phenomena.

This conclusion is based on the teaching of all the leading Catholic theologians and moralists of the day. Their doctrine.

both dogmatic and moral, constitutes the sacred science, whose principles, founded on God's own Revelation, are unchangeable and form the supreme standard of truth and morality. Hence we cannot accept the view of a recent Catholic writer who says that "the theological verdict on Spiritism should be adjusted to the new order of things." We rather think that the opposite course is far safer. Therefore modern scientific investigators, if they wish to steer clear of erroneous views, should be careful not to advance any statement that runs counter to revealed truth.

THIRD ARTICLE

The Serious Dangers of Spiritism.

Among the wise maxims taught mankind by their divine Master, Jesus Christ, is that which enables them to distinguish at once truth from error, right from wrong, and good from evil. It is the gospel test: "By their fruits you shall know them." Matthew vii, 16. We have the best possible authorities for resorting on occasion to this unerring principle, viz.: the dictate of reason, the unanimous consent of men, and the living voice of God's incarnate Son. By applying this infallible rule to the system of Spiritism and its agents we shall be able to know what we should think of them, and to determine what ought to be our attitude in their regard.

There are three most precious gifts placed by the beneficent Creator within the possession and reach of man. First, his just and correct relation to his Sovereign Maker and Lord through the knowledge and practice of religious, Christian faith. Secondly, the normal condition and operation of his mental faculties, intellect and free will, through which he can attend to and reach the end of his earthly existence, his heavenly appointed destiny, the fulfillment of God's holy will in this world, and the attainment of eternal happiness in the next. Thirdly, the healthy, faultless state of his moral conduct.

Here we pertinently ask: What is the influence of spiritistic communications on the three above mentioned gifts? God's authority, the verdict of reason and the sad lesson of experience compel us to say that it is fatal in the extreme to them all. In fact, Spiritism perverts in the individual experimenters and the mediums the teachings of Christian faith; it is a menace to the mental faculties, whose untrammeled exercise is needed to work out and secure our eternal salvation, it is utterly destructive of man's moral life.

The proofs we are about to allege will fully justify us in concluding that the complete wreck of men's highest gifts both natural and supernatural is the inevitable result of the practices of Spiritism in its worst phase. From their fruits then we shall learn what judgment we ought to form of the agents that produce them.

1. To begin with, what do the advocates of Spiritism teach us concerning Christianity and its Founder?

Let the Spiritists tell it themselves.

Sir Oliver Lodge: "The traditional teaching of Christianity will have to undergo a radical transformation."

Dr. Conan Doyle: "Christianity as a moral system I hold to be as pernicious as it is absurd."

Stainton-Moses: "Christ was a mere man. Through the revelation of the spirits we have lost a God-man; but we have gained a model man, all but divine."

Allan Karder: "The third revelation of the Son of God is that announced by the spirits who are the mouthpiece of heaven."

As shown in other spiritistic works, scarcely a truth of the Christian religion remains intact, for they reject the fall of man, the fact of redemption, Christ's miracles, His resurrection, the sacraments of the Church, the doctrine of eternal reward to the just, and everlasting punishment to the wicked, the inspiration of the Bible and other fundamental truths too numerous to mention.

Spiritism is a new Gospel superseding that of traditional Christianity. It is professedly the religion of the laity as opposed to sacerdotalism and the spiritual authority, which it antagonizes.

S. George Stock: "Christianity has spent its force, and Spiritism, another revelation, has succeeded it a revelation suited to the needs of the time."

It would be a huge mistake to believe that the new religion, destined to supplant Christianity, root and branch, forms a consistent, coherent, harmonious system of doctrines, for nothing is farther from the truth. All is contradiction, chaos and confusion. It is often found that what one spirit emphatically asserts, another just as emphatically denies. Nothing worse could be expected from the inmates of the infernal region, where, as the prophet Job tells us "no order but everlasting horror dwelleth," x. 22. There is, however, one point on which they all agree, their hatred of Christian truth.

After quoting the startling views of Spiritists on Christianity and its Founder, shall we undertake the task of confuting them? No, by no means, and this for two weighty reasons. First, because they are only copying from old and modern unbelievers or infidels assertions and assumptions refuted by both Catholic and Protestant apologists hundreds of times, as shown by the controversial works that fill the libraries of the civilized world. Secondly, because no one can be reasonably expected to answer charges unsupported by any proof. The ipse dixit of Sir Oliver Lodge and Dr. Conan Doyle, though they both hail from proud Albion, produces no conviction on the mind of the truth-seeking American people. When the Spiritists will offer us better credentials than the contradictory doctrines of their teachers, it will be time enough for us to submit them to a searching examination so as to ascertain what they are worth.

Speaking at the beginning of this article of the destructive character of the spiritistic religion, I said that it is calculated to pervert the principles of Christian faith in individuals. This is unhappily true of those who, in defiance of God's explicit prohibition, indulge in practices forbidden under the severest penalties. But as to historic Christianity, which, I maintain, is identical with Catholicism, the new-fangled revelation of the Spiritists, can no more affect it, than it can efface the sun from the heavens. This is the Christianity that has stood the test of the wise Jewish sage, Gamaliel who, nineteen hundred years ago, in Jerusalem defended the Apostles arrayed before the council, who were threatened with death for preaching the Christian faith, the Gospel of Jesus Christ. He spoke thus to the assembled judges: "I say to you, refrain from these men and let them alone; for if this work be of men, it will come to nought; but if it be of God, you cannot overthrow it." Acts, v. 38, 39.

Now after the lapse of nearly twenty centuries, which witnessed its unceasing combats and its perpetual victories, we may complete the argument and say: That work, the Christian religion, has not been overthrown, therefore it is the work of God. Applying the same test to the Spiritistic cult we do not hesitate to predict its downfall; it shall sooner or later come to nought, for it is the work not of God but of Satan. This new relevation ushered in by spirit messages, through the entranced mediums, is a gigantic delusion, a huge fraud imposed upon a world which has become estranged from Christ, and has lapsed into a new form of paganism.

All the truths of Christianity are so perfectly coherent, harmonious and consistent as to form one complete whole. None of them can be rejected without shaking the entire structure. Divine Revelation, God's masterpiece, resembles an arch so constructed that all the greater stones must be keystones. Displace one of them, and the whole fabric falls to pieces, and crumbles into dust. Hence it is a dangerous thing to meddle and tinker with revealed truth. It has been said that Christ is the solution of all difficulties. Deny his Divinity and all the difficulties and mysteries of the present life remain unsolved. Say, Jesus Christ is God, and all is intelligible. If He is not God, then Christianity is a fraud, a mockery, and its Founder the greatest impostor that ever appeared on the face of the earth. There is no other alternative, no middle ground.

Mr. Farmer, a staunch spiritist, in his work entitled, "A New Basis of Life", p. 36, is bold enough to assert that "Spiritualism (Spiritism) is a renewal of Christ's teachings, and a reappearance of the signs and wonders, which, He promised, should distinguish the true believer." Nothing is further from the truth than this arrogant pretention. Not one of the many miracles of Christ has ever been reproduced in any spiritistic performance, that is a genuine miracle, surpassing the power of all created agents, and requiring the intervention of God's omnipotence. Only such prodigies can bear testimony to heavenly revealed truth, and prove *that* religion to be divine in whose behalf they have been performed. Miracle accredit the miracle-worker and establish his credibility only when they are such as can be performed only by the finger of God. If they are such marvels as can be done by a created power, or by a lying spirit, they prove nothing as to the credibility of their author. Prodigies, therefore, though superhuman, which do not transcend the power of created intelligence, do not accredit the agent who performs them, particularly when the agent can and does lie and deceive. We entirely reject, therefore, the pretended identity between the doings of Spiritism and the Gospel miracles wrought by Christ as witnesses to his Divine Mission, and the truth of His message.

2. Another evil fruit of Spiritism.

The mental dangers attending spiritistic practices are recognized by men well qualified to speak with authority on the present subject. Dr. L. S. Forbes Winslow in his work on "Spritualistic Madness" (1877) wrote as follows:

"Thousands of unfortunate people are at present confined in lunatic asylums on account of having tampered with the supernatural." And quoting an American journal he goes on to say. "Not a week passes, in which we do not hear that some of these unfortunates destroy themselves by suicide, or are removed to a lunatic asylum. The mediums often manifest signs of an abnormal condition of their mental faculties, and among certain of them are found unequivocal indications of a true demoniacal possession. The evil spreads rapidly and it will produce in a few years frightful results."

But as all Christians must admit, by far the greatest danger to which spiritistic practitioners expose themselves, is that of incurring the eternal loss of their soul. For if insanity overtakes them when guilty of some grievous offense deserving endless punishment, and they were to depart from this life before recovering the normal use of reason, whose exercise is absolutely necessary for acts of worthy repentance, their doom is sealed.

Among the other evil effects attributed to spiritistic performances the following have been found to occur, particularly in the case of mediums: shattering of the bodily constitution, the impairing of the mental faculties, ever growing propensity to unlawful acts, paralyzing the energy of the will, whose power is gradually weakened, and is finally surrendered to the control of invisible agencies. Persistent temptations to suicide on the plea of joining the happy spirits in the great beyond, are also noted. Here again we conclude: if a tree is known by its fruit, what should we think of a system and of practices leading to such fatal consequences as are pointed out in hundreds of volumes on this subject and are summarized in the present article?

3. Immorality is another pernicious evil traceable to spiritistic doing. Dr. B. F. Hatch, an eminent American physician, former husband of the late Mrs. Cora V. Hatch, a once famous medium operating in several cities of the United States, writes: "The extensive opportunities, which I have had of studying the nature and results of Spiritism justify me, I think, in laying

just claims to being a competent witness on the matter in question. I have known many, whose integrity of character rendered them worthy examples to all around, but who on becoming mediums and giving up their individuality, that is the control of their will, also gave up every sense of honor and decency. There are thousands of high minded spiritists who will agree with me that it is no slander to say that the inculcation of no doctrine has ever shown such disastrous moral results as the practice of Spiritism, I stand appalled before the revelation of its awful realities. In my inquiries I have been able to count up over 70 mediums, most of whom have abandoned their conjugal relations."

Too much emphasis cannot be laid upon the wrecked homes, the ruined lives, the unbalanced minds, the blasted careers, and the lost peace and happiness of those who become involved in this most insidious of all modern perils, when all moral responsibility is deadened by indulgence in the lower passions and the operations of the will are well nigh paralyzed. It is a sad fact proved by experience that when the evil spirits take possession of human individuals, they employ them almost at will for their wicked purposes and compel them to write the foulest things, against which their miserable victims rebel but in vain. And yet we are expected to believe that it is by such disastrous methods that we are made the recipients of a new revelation superior to the Gospel of Christ. The answer to such hollow, proud boast has been given nearly twenty centuries ago by St. Paul when he thus wrote to the Galatians: "But though we, or an angel from heaven preach a Gospel to you besides that which we have preached to you, let him be anathema." Gal. 1. 8. And what should we say of this new Spiritistic Gospel preached not by an angel from heaven but by Satan and his rebel followers from the abyss of hell? Of all such as lend countenance to the satanic propaganda as mediums, experimenters and sitters spoke the Divine Master when He said, as we read in His Gospel: "You are of your father the devil, and the desires of your father you will do." John viii, 44.

I purposely refrain from mentioning other unsavory details lest I should offend the delicate sense of some readers. In this connection it is hardly necessary for me to assure the perusers of this paper that in alleging the above quotations no judgment of individual Spiritists is intended on our part. To judge men's secret actions belongs to God alone, and no man should dare to assume it. But the public systems or doctrinal teachings, to which men give adherence, are no secrets of the heart, and may therefore be examined and criticized.

We here recall the wise and charitable motto of St. Augustine: "Love men, but kill their errors." "Diligite homines, sed interficite errores."

In reliable works on the present subject I came across other startling accounts of the Spiritistic communications. In Utah, they defend polygamy. Where abortion and birth control are common, they declare such practices lawful and an hygienic obligation. At some sittings, in the presence of ladies, the spirits utter villainous, indecent words suggestive of evil. At times they have no other aim but to harm. As they themselves suffer, even when, by God's permission, they are out of hell, so they delight in tormenting men, whom they hate, and whose lot they envy for their being destined to fill in heaven the thrones left vacant by the rebel angels.

To prove once more that the invisible, free and intellectual agencies at work in the spiritistic seances are not the souls of the departed, but the wicked, fallen angels, the demons, I call the reader's attention to the following remarks: Can we reasonably suppose that the spirits of the dead, once our dear companions in life, take delight in deceiving the living? Is it conceivable that the souls of the departed, our dear relatives and friends will expose their surviving parents, their brothers and sisters to the irreligious, immoral and physical dangers described above?

Among the natural cravings of the human heart is the desire to know something certain about the unseen world. As Cardinal Gibbons well remarks: "The only serene questioning about the thrilling existence of the Hereafter is that of the man, whose Faith is sure, whose grasp of divine Revelation is firm and steady. There is no barrier between him and his God, no wall of mystery and uncertainty about his dear and noble dead." The Communion of Saints has always been an essential part of the Catholic Creed from the very dawn of Christianity. The Church firmly believes in the possibility of communication with the departed that have died in the Lord, whether they be already basking in the light of the beatific vision, or still detained in the purifying region of Purgatory. But such communing and interchange of spiritual benefits is carried on by the Faithful in a manner utterly at variance with the dangerous and often fatal methods of Spiritism.

Hence desire for knowledge concerning the departed and of the secrets of the great beyond does not at all disturb the earnest, devout Christian, who knows with certainty that his faith contains God's own Revelation regarding the future life and the immortality of his soul. But alas! the unhappy multitude that is destitute of the blessed, cheering hope founded on the religion of Jesus Christ, yearn for knowledge of the next world, for some means of bridging over the chasm that yawns between the living and the dead. They foolishly imagine that a satisfactory answer to their cravings is given by Spiritism. Poor creatures! They are the victims of a huge illusion, the sports of lying devils. They ask for the bread of truth, and they receive the stone of error. Our earnest prayer is that they may look elsewhere for reliable instruction and genuine consolation, that before it is too late, they may thus escape the fatal dangers of those, of whom St. Paul spoke in his first letter to Timothy: "Some shall depart from the faith, giving heed to spirits of error and doctrines of devils." I, IV, 1.

Authorities Cited

To assure the readers of my articles on Spiritism that the views expressed therein are thoroughly sound, orthodox and in full harmony with the teachings of modern Catholic philosophers and theologians approved by the Catholic Church, I here append the list of the authors I consulted. Several of them taught in the Papal Gregorian university of Rome. Their textbooks on philosophy, moral theology and canon law are used in the leading universities and seminaries of Europe and America. If the doctrine they teach on Spiritism, which I reproduced, is not orthodox and Catholic I should like to know what it is.

Philosophers—Schiffini, Palmieri, Urráburu, Ferretti.

Professors of Dogmatic Theology—Petavius, Perrone, Cardinal Mazzella.

Canonist—Ojetti.

Moral theologians—Ballerini, Buceroni, Genicot, Noldin, Lehmkuhl, Slater.

They are all members of the Society of Jesus, with whose works I happen to be fairly acquainted.

FOURTH ARTICLE

The Natural Endowments of the Fallen Angels.

These supplementary notes are published for the purpose of strengthening the arguments advanced in the three previous articles, issued in this journal, when the writer, not to trespass on the space allowed, found it necessary to be brief and concise.

Note 1. Necromancy and Spiritism Identical.

The attempt to hold intercourse with the inhabitants of the unseen world, is not, as some seem to imagine, a practice peculiar to these modern times. History proves that it was resorted to in all the epochs of antiquity, in civilized as well as in barbarous nations. It is only in the method of evoking those manifestations, that any difference can be said to exist between the practice of olden times and that of our days. The former superstition was designated under the name of Necromancy. This latter term, as defined in Standard dictionary (Funk & Wagnalls) shows its perfect identity with spiritism—"Necromancy is the art of foretelling the future by means of pretended communication with the dead. It is calling and invoking the aid of the devil. An effort to obtain information from the dead, or from demons." This superstitious practice was long ago proscribed both by the Church and the civil authorities of cultured nations. To establish the complete identity between Necromancy and spiritism we have but to compare the preceding definitions with the doctrine of the spiritists themselves, who hold that those wonderful communications are due to the souls of the dead, the departed human beings, that once inhabited this planet. Though, under the guidance of right reason and directed by the lessons of experience, the Spiritistic deception may be unmasked, yet it must be allowed that it is in historic Christian faith alone that we find the true standard by which the momentous problems presented by modern Spiritism can be fairly and adequately judged.

Note 2. The extraordinary and superhuman knowledge and power of angels.

To account for both the physical and intellectual feats exhibited in the spiritistic performances, we must briefly recall what orthodox theology teaches us regarding the endowment of angels.

As in men so in angels we must carefully distinguish the natural from the supernatural gifts bestowed on them by their Sovereign Creator and Supreme Benefactor. The chief supernatural gift conferred on the angelic multitude was sanctifying grace, which elevated them to a most intimate union with their Maker and fitted them for the heavenly happiness of the beatific vision, attainable on condition of their loyalty and submission to the Lord's will, the test of their fidelity. The precious gift of grace Lucifer and his followers forfeited forever by their sin and rebellion. But as to the mere natural gifts, constituting the very essence of pure spirits, they remained to them full and unimpaired. They are principally two, extraordinary knowledge and power far superior to those possessed by even the most gifted men. As to knowledge, they possess such penetration as to be able by a single glance to take in the whole field of science both physical and rational along with its numerous branches. However vast may be the comprehension of the angelic mind, it is restricted by two most important limits.

First, it cannot know with certainty future events that depend on the free action of God or man.

Second, it can have no sure knowledge of man's inner thoughts, called the secrets of the hearts.

Hence utterances on such matters, often heard in spiritistic seances, are mere wild guesses or downright falsehoods intended by the lying spirits to deceive the illuded experimenters and the assembled sitters.

The Formidable Power of Angels

A very striking proof is the event related in Holy Scripture, when one single angel slew in one night 185,000 soldiers of the Assyrian army of the impious King Sennacherib, who had defied the God of Israel to save Jerusalem from destruction. IV Kings XIX, 35. Sincere Christian believers have nothing to fear from the power of the good angels, our divinely appointed guardians and protectors, of whom St. Paul writes: "Are they not all ministering spirits sent to minister for them who shall receive the inheritance of salvation?" Hebrew I, 14. We can have no surer guarantee of assistance against the conspiracy of demons than the fear and love of God, of Him whose tenderness for His loyal servants is infinite and whose power is almighty.

On the other hand, as Christian doctrine teaches us, the wicked angels, the sworn enemies of mankind, impelled by their hatred of God, and the envy of men, are ever ready to make use of their astounding power against us. They are, however, subject to the full control of divine omnipotence for the maintenance and preservation of the physical, moral, social and spiritual order of the world. Hence the devil's power also has its limitations, which have been providentially fixed by Almighty God, and beyond which it is impossible for him to act. But if men, in defiance of the peremptory divine prohibition, wilfully and of their own accord place themselves within the reach of the evil influence of Satan and his satellites, the wicked angels, by meddling with spiritistic practices, all know who is to blame if they fall victims to such dreadful calamities as have been described in previous articles. When, therefore, we take into account the prodigious knowledge and power naturally possessed by the fallen angels, the demons, we need not be surprised at the astounding physical and intellectual wonders displayed in spiritistic meetings; remarkable wonders indeed, which can in no wise be attributed to the presence and action of the dead for the all-sufficient reason that they possess neither the knowledge nor the power needed to produce them.

Note 3. The several forms of Occultism.

Though designated by different names, yet they are more or less superstitious practices, and as such they all fall under the ban of condemnation. They are as follows: Mesmerism, magnetism, hypnotism, the ouija board or the French planchette and modern Spiritism. All their effects, which cannot be accounted for by the action of natural forces, must be reckoned as preternatural, and therefore due to the agencies of invisible, free intelligent beings. These beings, it has been shown, are no other than the wicked angels, the demons. This is precisely the principle on which the Catholic Church bases the reason of the several condemnations issued by its authority. In fact in a decree published June 25, 1840, the cardinals of the Holy Office speak thus: "The application of purely physical principles or means to things or effects that are really supernatural, in order to explain these on physical grounds, is nothing else than unlawful and heretical deception."

Here we pertinetly ask: What are the effects that are really supernatural, and which, according to the mind of the Catholic

Church, cannot be accounted for **naturally,** and require therefore the intervention of preternatural agents for their production? We find the answer in another decree of the Holy Office issued July 30th, 1850. They are chiefly the following:

"To claim to see things naturally invisible; to answer questions on religion; to evoke and consult the souls of the dead; to detect things distant beyond the reach of human capacity; to receive answers to things or questions naturally ignored." Are not these the very things done in the spiritistic seances? Therefore whoever holds that these and similar effects can be obtained by the application of physical agencies or forces, that is by purely natural means, cannot evade the condemnation of the Holy Office, which in its decrees proscribes the above spiritistic practices and phenomena as superstitious, diabolical, heretical, and as a deception absolutely unlawful. See Tanquery, vol. 1, p. 321.

The Second Council of Baltimore (1866) declares that some at least of the manifestations of Spiritism are to be ascribed to Satan's intervention. What the Church condemns in spiritism is not the mere use of physical means for obtaining natural effects, but what in it is superstitious with its evil consequences, religious, mental and moral.

Note 4. Immortality and Spiritism.

Immortality, the cornerstone of religion and morality, has been fiercely assailed and denied by many, not because it is not solidly proved, but because its opponents, reckless in their private conduct, dread the awful responsibility, which it entails in the endless world to come. Its truth is indeed the joy of the just and the terror of the wicked. Besides being divinely revealed, it is the inevitable postulate of reason when fairly consulted. It is, moreover, the universal belief of mankind—a belief all the more striking since it persists in spite of the violent opposition from the alluring passions of men. All accurate thinkers in all times have admitted this rational tenet, and it is for this reason that the schoolmen in their demonstration of the soul's immortality never gave any prominence to the argument derived from the spiritistic phenomena observed in the past. Modern spiritism pretends to furnish an incontestable new proof of immortality and future life; a claim to be by all means rejected, for its validity rests, after all, upon their theory that the communications come from disembodied spirits—a theory which we proved to be absolutely untenable. Hence it is not true to say that spiritism has dealt the deathblow to materialism, for if the doctrine of spiritism were the only argument for the existence of future life, materialism, instead of being crushed, would still triumph. As the history of philosophy testifies, the deathblow of materialism has been given long years ago by the works of Catholic psychologists under the leadership of the prince of philosophers and theologians, St. Thomas Aquinas. As Dr. John Quackenbos well said: "The real proof of immortality is not to be sought in the vaporings of spiritism."

Note 5. Authorities advocating the Catholic View of Spiritism.

Besides the Catholic philosophers, theologians, canonists and moralists quoted in the third article, the following authors are added.

1. Modern Spiritism and the New Black Magic, by J. Godfrey Raupert.

2. Sermons on Modern Spiritualism, by A. V. Muller.

3. Spiritism Unveiled, by Rt. Rev. B. L. Lanslot, O. S. B.

4. The Unseen World, by A. M. Lepicier, O. S. M.

5. Brownson's Review, The Spirit Rapper, Vol. IX.

6. The Homiletic Monthly, November, 1919.

7. The Ecclesiastical Review, June, 1918; January, 1920; April, 1920.

8. The Irish Monthly, January, 1920.

9. Perils of Spiritualism, by Herbert Thurston in Studies, an Irish Review.

10. Spiritualism, by Mgr. Benson.

11. Spiritism and Modern Satanism, by F. F. Cookley.

12. Abridgment of Moral Theology, by Cardinal D'Annibale.

13. Synopsis of Dogmatic Theology, by A. Tanquery, S. S.

14. Moral Theology, by Scavini.

15. Civiltá Cattolica, a fortnightly Roman review conducted by the Jesuit Fathers, 1864-1865.

Note 6.

Men of scientific attainments and upright character, after

long and careful investigation, declare that certain physical and psychical phenomena of spiritism witnessed by them cannot be explained by any cause known to science. Hence they freely admit that they surpass both nature's and man's powers and are therefore preternatural, due to free, intellectual agencies of a malignant character, as revealed by spiritistic results. They therefore fully justify the attitude of the Catholic Church in denouncing the pernicious influence of spiritistic practices, and in warning men against the physical, religious and moral dangers attending them.

Postscript

Mr. O. P. Thornton, of Saratoga, referring to my articles, thanks me for my admission of the truth of many of the phenomena of modern Spiritism. I feel grateful for his courteous acknowledgment and I take occasion to reiterate the statement that, allowing for the exposure, at times, of trickery and jugglery, many of the marvels witnessed in the spiritistic performances are real, genuine, authentic facts, which cannot be called in question by any sensible man. But, on the other hand, I cannot subscribe to his assertion that "it matters little to logical investigators what cause they assign."

Old Virgil does not agree with him, for he said:

"Felix qui potuit rerum cognoscere causas." (Happy is he who could know the causes of things.") Georgica II, 490.

The chief thing in spiritism is to know the cause, that is to detect the real agents producing those marvelous feats. This I have endeavored to find out in the course of my articles, which led me logically to the conclusion that evil results must be traced to an evil cause, and this is no other than devilish intervention.

As a very fitting conclusion of our discussion we here quote from the Monitor (April 3, 1920), Bishop Turner's warning on Spiritism. Whoever has followed the trend of our articles will be candid enough to admit that our views, however imperfectly stated, are in full agreement with those of his Lordship who formerly held with honor the chair of philosophy in the Catholic University at Washington, D. C.

The Human Soul's Immortality and Spiritism.

Buffalo, March 19, 1920.—Bishop William Turner, of Buffalo, in a statement given out on Saturday, explained the attitude of the Catholic Church toward the nefarious doctrine of Spiritism which is spreading rapidly in the United States and England. He cautioned the faithful against the tremendous spiritistic propaganda which is now being carried out in this country, as well as against the ouija board, or planchette, by means of which a great many unsophisticated persons first get interested in Spiritism and are gradually led astray.

Bishop Turner declared that the Church has forbidden communication with evil spirits from apostolic times and has always warned against false prophets. Referring to the evil effects of "The New Revelation", the Bishop said the "messages" received by the exprimenter in Spiritism, though apparently harmless at first, soon become sinister, and gradually undermine his religious faith and destroy his moral character.

"These messages," Msgr. Turner declared, "at their best are trivial, irrelevant, flippant; at their worst, they are immoral, irreverent, atheistic or even blasphemous. They often cause dissensions in families, undermine faith in God and tend to subvert established moral standards. They are, apparently, 'the evil fruit of an evil tree.' They cannot come from any good source."

Concerning the position of the Catholic Church toward Spiritism, Bishop Turner said:

"Ever since apostolic times, the Church has forbidden commerce of all kinds with evil spirits, and has warned the faithful against false prophets. As to the current practice of Spiritism, the Church has forbidden Catholics to assist at spiritistic communications or manifestations, even when these bear the appearance of being honest and pious, even though one tacitly or expressly excludes the intention of dealing with evil spirits. And the effects that usually follow from the practice of Spiritism amply justify this prohibition. Physicians can testify to these effects, and quite recently, I believe, it was proposed in California to forbid by law the use of the ouija board because of the number of cases in which that practice led to insanity.

"The Church would welcome scientific proof of immortality, but she would be slow to accept proof that merely claims to be scientific. The immortality of the soul is a philosophical, not a scientific truth. The proofs of it from reason, from consciousness, from the existence of the moral order, and so forth, are honored in the traditional philosophy of the Catholic schools. But as these are technical proofs, they do not appeal to the untrained mind with all their force.

"The Church, therefore, in her preaching and practice, has stressed the fact of immortality on Scriptural grounds, on the strength of facts which are known to be true, and while she would undoubtedly, like her Founder, wish 'all men to come to a knowledge of the truth,' she does not believe that mediums are the divinely chosen means of bringing about a universal belief in immortality."

Works by the Same Author:

CHRISTIAN APOLOGETICS [Two Vol.]....... $2.50

THE FUTURE LIFE.......................... $2 50

FOR SALE AT THE

O'CONNOR COMPANY

341 Stockton Street, San Francisco, California.

In Course of Preparation:

THE LAST THINGS OF MAN AND OF THE WORLD.
NOVISSIMA HOMINIS ET NOVISSIMA MUNDI.

Printed by Libri Plureos GmbH in Hamburg, Germany